Not the
IT Infrastructure Library

I name this baby Norman.Nerd@AOL.COM

Dedicated to technoids everywhere, bless 'em.

BJ & PW

Acknowledgements

Those who bought the original 'Not the Infrastructure Library', thus encouraging the authors to make a second attempt.

All the souls who provided the raw input for the characters appearing in this tome.

Don Page for cash for inclusion in the acknowledgments; George Bush for reminding Mugabe that election fixing is neither big or clever; John Stewart for cash for being left out of the mickey-taking and also for suggestions.

Sjoerd Hulzinga, Louk Peters & Aidan Lawes for suggestions and comments.

Published by : *it*SMF UK Ltd.

Concept & Text : Giggle Productions
Brian Johnson (words) & Paul Wilkinson (words and cartoons)

ISBN 0-9524706-7-5

Layout by The Hieroglyph Group
Printed by Thamesdown Colour 4/02

Foreword

Recently, here in the home of good practice, the poor performance of the wide and local area networks was discussed together with the reasons for the failure of the IT people to forecast problems.

'Ah well', said the IT director, 'we don't monitor performance because one of you lot will always tell us when response time is awful'.

And I once said to Brian that his less than diplomatic methods of informing people of their inability to manage IT were somewhat harsh…

Well, perhaps this latest treatise on worst practice will help. Again I must point out that it is a concern that this book is based on real life and you will no doubt be surprised to recognise situations that exist in your own environment. I would also point out that at least this time the guys have left me alone, choosing instead to lampoon other people who may be known to you. It was worth the money.

John Stewart, OGC

Introduction

Business and IT: Mis-Alignment

The rapid pace of technological advancement! The increased potential for new business benefits that ICT offers! The scale and pace of business change! Globalisation! Mergers and acquisitions... All of these incredibly boring things get in the way of going to the strip club and visiting the brown café for a, erm, herbal cigarette. Or cross dressing and singing songs about Marlene (if you are German). Or killing people if you are a computer programmer in Hicksville, CA.

And of course, advancements place additional demands and expectations on the ICT organisation and the relationship between the business and IT. The boring thingies, that is. Unfortunately, the way in which these business & IT developments and the necessary decision making is aligned, or should we say MIS-aligned, means that many organisations are not able to move quickly enough to take advantage of the opportunities. A good thing too for those of us in IT who are far too busy annoying users to be bothered with that sort of stuff.

This book examines some of the key areas in which this mis-alignment should be maintained. It does not, however, provide a guide either to transvestitism or serial killing, as these are against our principles, though for the right money our principles can be changed.

Chapter one: The Business problem

This chapter should actually be entitled 'The Business is the problem'.

There is no doubt that information systems and leading edge applications can offer significant business benefits. Faster time-to-market of products through the use of computer aided design systems; more efficient, streamlined business operations with enterprise resource planning; higher quality services to customers through customer relationship management systems; faster and more accurate analysis and decision making through the use of management information systems; the list goes on.

It is the job of all IT professionals (IT service managers, applications developers,and maintainers, some women) to minimise the impact of change. On us. We must work together as we have failed to do in the past, to slow things down to snail pace and to improve on what we do best (allow budgets to over run, deadlines to be missed by decades and projects miserably to fail). Of course we managed this by not working together to some extent, but if we unite, then business will have to work even harder to get us to do what they need.

For far too long now, business executives have been passing all the blame onto the IT organisation. Piss poor IT service and unreliable systems are not always the only excuse for the lack of benefit realisation. A significant portion of the blame lies squarely with business executives. Lucky for us.

These executives give speeches about the power of Information and Communications Technology and announce huge investments in leading edge technology solutions. They launch corporate-wide roll-outs of desktop infrastructures and applications environments tailored to meet the needs of all business functions.

However it is these executives that are the last ones to embrace the technology. They ignore it themselves and hope that the rest of the organisation will become IT literate on their behalf.

One leading American bank recognised this problem and decided it was time to make senior executives IT literate. They launched a program called Necessary Executive Reshaping Degree - three called three months in which business executives were trained in the use of the company software applications. Creating a boardroom full of NERDS. No change there then!

...really I mean it... it can be used for more than just the clock and calculator functions!...

B-2B or not B-2b That is the Question (Fred Shakespeare)

Business managers the world over have suddenly seen the light; any ICT-related word beginning with the letter '**e**' as in '**e**'-business, means business. ICT can actually deliver real business benefits (er, we mean money).

It can be used to **enable** new business models to realise **enormous** cost savings and **explosive** revenue growth and **engender enduring** customer satisfaction and loyalty. We would be inclined to say 'What a heap of **excrement**' but business won't listen to us. No. They have suddenly been converted through two sources of **enlightenment.**

• Every single business or management magazine in the world declaring that e-business is the next holy grail of ICT as a new business model. These publications act as a hypnotic form of subliminal advertising - "**earn** money ... sign up now before it's too late". Business executives leap onto the e-wagon with the sweet naivete of those brain deficient individuals that respond to adverts declaring "send us $5 and we'll send YOU information that will make YOU a MILLIONAIRE!!!".
• E-business acts as a sort of pied piper **enchantment** drawing just about every business and management consultant out of the woodwork, every one displaying the **ethical** traits of those mid-western Quack doctors selling **elixirs** of life and patented cure-alls.

In responding as they do to these enticements, business executives display the same maturity traits as the IT managers in the eighties and early nineties.

For the IT manager it was the letter '**X**' that seemed to be irresistible. 'Give me some of that client/server technology and those sexy operating systems that all have an '**X**' somewhere in the name 'Uni**X**','Linu**X**','Xini**X**' and 'Bollo**X**'.' Never mind the consequences.

IT managers have since suffered the wrath of business managers decrying escalating maintenance costs and a mass of systems, applications and databases that refuse to communicate with one another making ICT about as flexible as certain fundamentalist sects' attitude to women (actually quite similar to the view that we in IT have of women in IT). IT managers are still smarting from the pain and have learnt their lessons the hard way, having been dragged back to reality by business managers.

Business managers are now crying out for 'web-enabled' business. "Give me an internet. No, better still make it two. Give me some e-business, some e-procurement, some e-commerce, let me sell over the internet, let the customers order directly with us through on-line transactions."

Never mind the consequences. Often in their haste to get to market with their e-solution, they forget to integrate back-office processes into the total solution offering, the so-called fulfilment side of e-business ending up with a set of pissed-off customers. The promise of guaranteed customer satisfaction and loyalty having disappeared about as fast as the e-business consultants. In this new economy there is nothing so fickle as a cyber consumer who when disgruntled, will simply take his 'click' somewhere else.

The cry of the business managers is now 'Blood**E** hell!'. They are being brought back into line by their Customers.

But...

Once business managers decide they want the benefits of IT they start asking tricky questions:

'Is IT capable of delivering the benefits?'

The IT manager should be more inclined to ask the question *'Is the business capable of using IT to realise business benefits?'* The diagram illustrates the the business & IT view of one another's capabilities.

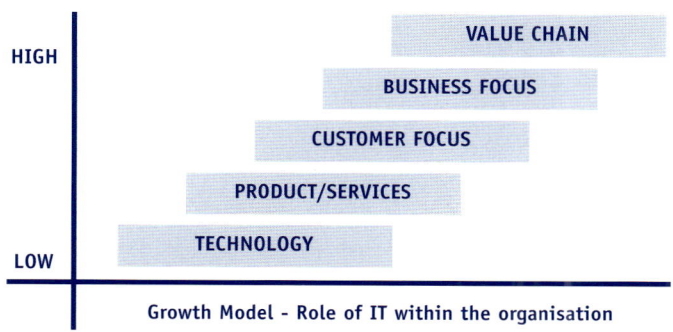

Growth Model - Role of IT within the organisation

The following table expands the diagram and looks at the maturity of the IT organisation from the IT and the business perspective. It assumes (always dangerous) that if IT and the business focus only on technology then it is a pretty bloody immature organisation and that's where we want to work. If however they focus on the value chain that IT can enable, well unless they screwed up on e-business (very likely) then we will stay in the sandpit thanks very much.

	IT	*Business*
Technology	IT bods are technoids who run infrastructures. They are shadowy figures, living in the dark and rarely seek company outside of their own. They speak in technobabble.	IT is far too complex for us, so long as it keeps blipping and beeping and the payroll gets printed. Leave the technoids to do whatever it is they do.
Product service	IT starts to leave its cave and realise that it needs the business to keep feeding it with money for new IT. The explosion of the PC and desktop goodies was characteristic of this evolutionary growth. IT spawned the existence of a strange breed of beings known as 'users'.	Business people start asking for technology to play with. Why should IT get all the fun? They get a PC on every desk, each user trying to outdo the others with unique and funny screen savers. Some even know how to get the calculator function to work.
Customer	IT is driven by complaints and sudden business realisation that IT eats money. Costs become heavily scrutinised. IT must provide some kind of service. *"If we're paying all this money shouldn't we expect it to at least work?"*. IT becomes aware of a breed of creatures even more dangerous than 'users'. This breed is known as the 'customer'. Basically, a 'customer' is a 'user' with money.	Users start moaning when IT doesn't work. They figure out how to use IT in their daily work. You really can do more than just play games. Now that they want to use it, they need to know how it is supposed to work. They now want somebody they can phone to ask all their bloody stupid questions.

A help desk would be nice! |

	IT	Business
Business	*IT* IT struggles to maintain its existence. It is expected to have a strategy. Worse still, one that is somehow aligned to the business. IT must prove that all those business consultants and experts are lying and that IT really does have a strategy and it does include the word business.	*Business* Business consultants and Gurus are a new breed of beings who start spouting buzzwords and catch phrases such as knowledge management, customer relationship management, business process re-engineering and are telling the business world that all their problems are caused by IT. Or lack of it, if that gets more money.
Chain	IT at last gets back its position of strength by taking ownership of the internet and web and going back into a cave. They start grunting and spouting once again technobabble such as html and xml in an effort to convince the business to leave them alone and let them get on with it again And give them more money.	e-business is dropped into just about every business conversation by just about every business manager so that they can pretend they know what they're talking about. Surfing for free games and naughty pictures creates a revolution in the business understanding of something called the internet.

We've decided to put toilet paper in the Director's printer… that way his reports will be useful for at least one thing!…

Chapter Two: Business & IT alignment

The Business perspective

From the CEO point of view, an explosion of business-related media attention has caused a reawakening of interest in Business and IT alignment (a CEO will use words like 'Business and IT alignment' and as we are CEO material, so do we. In fact we have used it twice, because when addressing the great unwashed (that's you), CEO-material types (that's us) often say things twice to illustrate that they can remember their lines).

- Some sigh and shake their heads *"Another consultancy inspired catchphrase designed to help promote a new range of useless advice and guidance",*
- or *"another excuse for developing a whole host of conferences and seminars all designed to tie up a business manager's time, and at the same time remove vast sums of shareholders' well earned profits".*

So is it just a hype? No, no, no, no, no, no, no, no, no, no, no, no, no, no, no, no, no, no, no, no, no, no, no, no.

Yes. It is.Mostly.

The IT Director was careful not to use the words 'disappear up your own backside' when explaining his new strategy

But for some business managers the penny has dropped. In the "new economy" characterised by the runaway train of adolescent, web-focused e-business solutions, with more and more businesses chasing the promise of globalised markets, more and more businesses facing the harsh reality of customers demanding individualisation and personalisation, customers suddenly find themselves with a massive choice of, of, of, loads of, of, of, *things*, through a simple click of a button...

It is now clear to all that the internet and e-business is not all hype. It is in fact mostly pornography (but that's another story) and bankruptcy (but we will leave that alone too).

Business will, and must, be supported, in fact *enabled*, by technology (it is our job after all; but we must ensure that enabling is governed by us, not them). It means that business & IT alignment is something that requires a little more serious thought. And given that IT has generally failed fairly spectacularly in the past to enable even bits of paper to be printed in remotely numerical sequence then it is time to start asking some probing questions.

*"How well do we **really** align use of IT with business needs and opportunities?".*

"Is IT really an enabler?".

And of course, the perennial favourite when such questions arise, *"How the bloody hell do I get early retirement before they find out the answers to the above?".*

The IT perspective (i.e., the right one)

From the IT director's point of view, now is the moment of truth. Will the business blame IT for the fact that the business has had its head buried in a bucket of sand for the last 10 years?

No, no, no, no, no, no, no, no, no, no, no, no, no, no, no, no, no, no, no, no, no, no, no, no.

Yes. It will. Entirely.

And with some justification;

a) because someone should have told them
b) because IT had its head up its backside for that period (when it wasn't contemplating its navel, or downloading porn)

Some see alignment as a dangerous trend that is making IT visible to business managers. More and more business managers are starting to take serious interest in IT and ask awkward questions. For example;

"Do we get value for our money?",
"Does IT add benefit to the business?",
"Where can I find advice about cross dressing?"
"If IT really is so important perhaps we should get an IT provider that knows what they are doing?!!? "...

"Next thing you know," declare indignant IT directors, *"is that they'll even start insisting they own IT and that they should decide what the business does with it!!"*

Er, yes.

Others see it as the dawning of a new era in which IT will claim it's rightful place, enabling megalomaniac IT managers to take over the company. So no change there then.

Our aims as IT professionals must be to ensure that IT is put back on the pedestal on which it so rightly belongs…

After all……it wasn't for NOTHING that the first words were "Let there be IT!"

Why should we be concerned? The key players will actually have to start talking to each other - sharing interests, swapping 'Survival' and 'Guns and Ammo' magazines, listing addresses for those intriguing web sites populated by gymnastic ladies (or men, if that is your preference) and interesting variations of one fairly specific activity.

And here lies one of the major problems in business & IT-alignment. No, not the porn stupid. The fact that Business and IT don't understand each other.

Before we get bogged down in business & IT alignment models and CONsultancy buzzwords and catchphrases that supposedly clarify the dilemma (As if; were they to clarify things the CONsultants would be out of work): let's look at an analogy.

Business and the IT service provider are like a long-married couple. The two partners have been together a long time. They accept each others faults and failings. They commonly complain "My partner doesn't understand me". They bemoan their fate and accept a relationship less than ideal for both parties. They flirt with other service providers. They have the occasional lunch. Even dinner. One thing leads to another and before you know it, they are in a hotel room somewhere, with a bottle of wine, the curtains are shut and then slowly…. bloody hell, sorry about that.

'I blame the American family values of the 60s for today's business & IT alignment problems'(Bill Gates (did not say that, we made it up, sorry.))

Business and IT marriages can be seen as a throwback to the 60s where the men (business) went out to work and did the important things while the women (IT) stayed at home to look after the completely unimportant things such as technology (hoovering, using the cooker, the washing machine, the dish washer etc; then, in the massive

amounts of free time they had created through use of these labour saving devices, they slept or did something called *'Bringing up the children'*, that took up, well, minutes we suppose. Then they sat around preparing what were known as 'jobs to do' lists that were handed to the returning men. The lists were designed to illustrate that even more technology was needed in order to allow more time for the women to rest. Men generally resisted, as it was obvious to them that no further increase in female leisure time was necessary).

In the sixties, these lists acted as an early form of contraception, but otherwise were not much use. Clearly women just should not have so much free time really, and here lie the roots of today's problems with business use of more technology.

So we move on to the present day. We men now realise that some technology is good; play stations, guns and so on. And women are back where they belong; working for us.

Some business managers refuse to accept the changing role, shouting, "Women know about technology. Let them do the typing. Men should just tell everyone what to do and forget the typing".

Of course this is true. But they have forgotten that men now use different technology; indeed they love it. And that women should now be occupied on more suitable tasks, such as making the coffee. And they have forgotten that men have asserted themselves as the real decision makers.

When the wife allows it, that is.

Bonding

Business managers go off to business seminars and conferences where they get together with like-minded folk and down the odd glass or eight of wine and complain that their IT partners just don't understand them. IT managers go off to IT conferences with like-minded IT managers where they down the odd 5 or 6 buckets of beer in the bar afterwards, talk about knitting and bringing up the kids (ie, the wife bringing up the kids), moan about their business partners and agree to get together for their version of a Tupperware party (technology conferences and show cases) where they can look at the latest technology gadgets without inviting those 'business people' along.

And then they drift further apart. And that's the way we want to keep it.

IT bonding; the rules

The IT directors go off and invest in some nice looking IT that looks pretty (this is why cyber sex is so popular with PC-nerds; these people actually find aesthetically pleasing certain aspects of computer screens, keyboards, printers, anglepoise lamps, desks, chair legs and so on). If it beeps a lot and more often than not doesn't do what the business needs to do, then it is considered perfect. In this way, IT can keep control of every aspect of the mis-alignment process.

So what are we IT superstars supposed to do?

Assess the business use of IT. Just about every business on the planet seems to be busy with some kind of change. Change is no longer the exception; it's becoming the norm. Therefore the first thing a business manager needs to do is to change something. Anything. Then as they will fail to understand the type of growth, the sort of change and the possible benefits that IT could provide in helping realize the change, they can pay handsomely for an IT expert to advise them.

Understanding your role in the problem...

Here is a popular model we can use (actually, it is not popular at all, but Paul likes it and I owe him money).

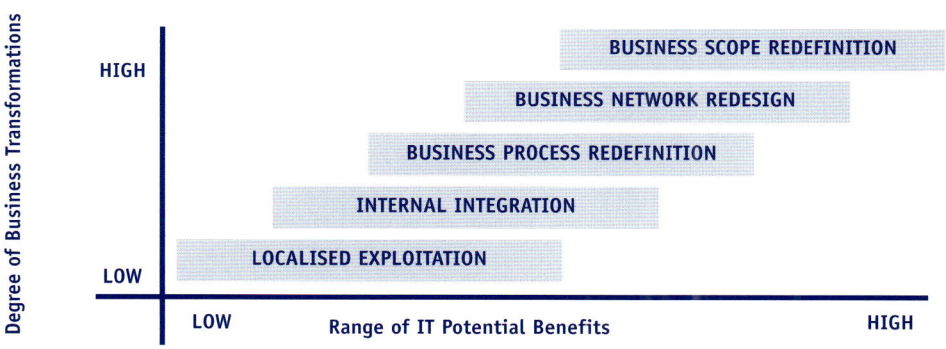

All business changes can be placed somewhere on this grid. You can demonstrate your complete understanding of things, promise lots and then simply fail to deliver anything on the basis that you were only discussing the *potential* benefits of IT and the higher and more complex the business change the greater the range of *potential* IT benefits; and by the way, if both parties fail to communicate properly, how were you to know they actually wanted something when they didn't actually say, so how will the benefits ever be articulated, let alone realised? So there!

The CIO

The sudden realisation by business managers that IT is pretty important after all and bloody hell, look at the morons we've got running it, causes them to realise that maybe a sort of marriage counsellor is a good idea. Somebody to build a bridge between IT and the business. This is the role of the CIO. It used to mean 'Career is Over' and wise business managers wouldn't touch the function with a bargepole.

Page was the obvious choice for CIO when the CEO pointed out that he displayed no ability for strategic thinking, ran about like a headless chicken and could not spell 'Information'

However, the increased business use of IT as a strategic instrument (their words) is picking up pace and the development of the CIO is not going quickly enough. They think we CIO types aren't developing our business skills quickly enough.

Cheeky monkeys.

Business managers have rushed headlong into e-business forgetting that the new business environment is inherently more risky. A key success factor according to industry experts and consultants, (and who the hell ever got rich believing that lot) is a new approach to the tolerance and management of risk within companies. Not just the risk of doing it, but also the risk of not adopting e-business. The CONsultants advice is to stop fooling around with a web-presence but to invest in real, money making e-business (explains the success of the dotcoms does it not, fnaar, fnaar) and manage risks appropriately.

Common mantras are: 'What is the risk if organisations do not heavily involve the back-office processes in e-solutions? What is the risk posed by the current level of IT-capability? Can we expect IT overnight to become e-competent?'

"...I ordered it over 20 minutes ago."

Betts ordered a Ham and Mushroom Pizza over the internet and needed technical support to identify where it was stuck in his PC

"Don't give me any more of this 'critical path analysis' crap Johnson... just point this thing towards America and put your foot down!..."

S.S. TITANIC

Of course they can't, we work in IT and will make bloody sure it fails. For *e*-competent read incompetent.

Of course, we can bet hard cash that all these CONsultants have a risk model that can help you and which can be purchased at an advantageous price.. Or an ITIL book. Or an idea that they are developing as an ITIL book. Or that they wrote all of the ITIL books and therefore they should be heeded.

Applications manglement

In a recent European study, it was revealed that more than 80% of IT projects are over time and/or budget and/or fail to deliver expected benefits. A leading research group report revealed that less than 5% of IS solutions actually get into and survive live usage.

Well. We don't wish to crow, but that proves IT is working just the way we like it. And that they can tell us the bleeding obvious.

We have already seen that the business must take part of the praise, but it is the developers that deserve the medal of honor. We thought that we in IT service management were good at delivering piss-poor service and getting away with it for all these years. Compared to IS development teams and programmers we are rank amateurs; we have a lot to learn from these unsung heroes.

OGC positions this incompetence in the ITIL publication relating to Applications Management. We call it *Applications Manglement*. Developers can take a set of defined business requirements and functional needs, pass it through their manglement process and come up with something altogether different and of no use to man, beast or user (the creature at the end of the evolutionary chain).

Once these loosely integrated pieces of software code, held together by bits of programming string and sellotape, get into the production environment and fall apart at the first sight of a user, we in IT service management inevitably end up taking the blame. And of course that keeps us in a job. Thanks again guys!

They call their process the application life-cycle. We call it the applications nose-dive. It looks like this:

An IT support person once explained; debugging is the process of removing bugs, programming is the process of putting them in. And that keeps everyone in IT happy.

Programming today is a race between software engineers striving to build bigger and better idiot-proof programs and the universe trying to produce bigger and better idiots. And so far the universe is winning.

A user once described a program as a magic spell cast over your computer that turns your input into error messages. Potter, that was his name. Harold. Right pillock.

IT projects & the business

Managers should take notice of Gartner trends and reports. They predict that by 2003, 70% of enterprises will institutionalise systematic assessment of IT-related projects, formalising guidelines for project approval, continuation, suspension and cancellation.

Swines.

As we have already mentioned, ICT project performance comes in for a lot of stick. If the business starts getting all stroppy about IT projects, IT managers should make a show of implementing PRINCE2 or an equivalent recognised project management method. Let PIDs (Project Initiation Documents) fly around like loose shrapnel and watch the business managers fly for cover when they realise they have to become involved in project steering. They'll soon give it up as a bad joke.

Managing risk with very big arrows

In our first book, we taught IT professionals to use words such as 'customers' and 'service' to help con er...convince the business community that we were customer-focused.

Now that we are expected to be a business-focussed IT organisation, we must start using words and phrases such as;

'effective and efficient delivery of IT services'.

Especially in the presence of customers. Words like efficient and effective make them feel happy and excite them, because they begin with the letter 'e' and we've already seen the hypnotic attraction to words beginning with 'e'.

We have recently come to the conclusion that we in IT should actually be grateful for ITIL. One of its great benefits is that it has given us a ready-made slogan to chant at the customers, for ITIL declares that it will *help us provide efficient and effective IT service delivery!*

IT managers don't need to worry about *implementing* ITIL. Just make a mission statement or vision statement (more sexy buzzwords that business managers like) containing these words and watch them roll over like pet dogs.

Business managers feel comfortable when we use words like 'service' and 'customers' and 'REAL needs'. This sounds like we care about them and understand their needs and are there to serve them. What they need is a good kicking, but putting that in a mission statement isn't very diplomatic. 'Efficient' and 'effective' are good because nobody knows what they really mean or how to measure them. Let's consider what these catch-all words really mean to us.

Effective

'Producing or capable of producing an intended result'

We in IT find we are very effective. Our intended result is to have users live in fear of us and to be thankful that when they log-in their files are still there. When we change something it stays changed. Yes, we can say with all sincerity that we strive to be effective.

Efficient

'The ratio of the effective or useful output to the total input in any system'.

In other words *'bullshit in bullshit out'*. As we declared in our first publication, "IT users deserve the Infrastructure they get".

Their input is:
- Inability to make up their minds about what they really want
- Inability to remember a password if there is a weekend in between when they last logged in and the current time
- Thinking that if they press F1 somebody will turn up and help them
- Business managers who stare at a mouse wondering what sort of beast it is or wondering why that thing on their desk that looks like a television hasn't got a remote control on it or why it can't receive CNN.

ITIL in the new economy

Traditional IT service improvement programmes focussed primarily on implementing the ITIL service support processes in which the users were lucky to get a human voice to insult them rather than a recorded message when they called the help desk.

Or we implemented change management procedures requiring them to actually sign their names on bureaucratic request forms (which we either binned or kept merely to be used as evidence against them.)

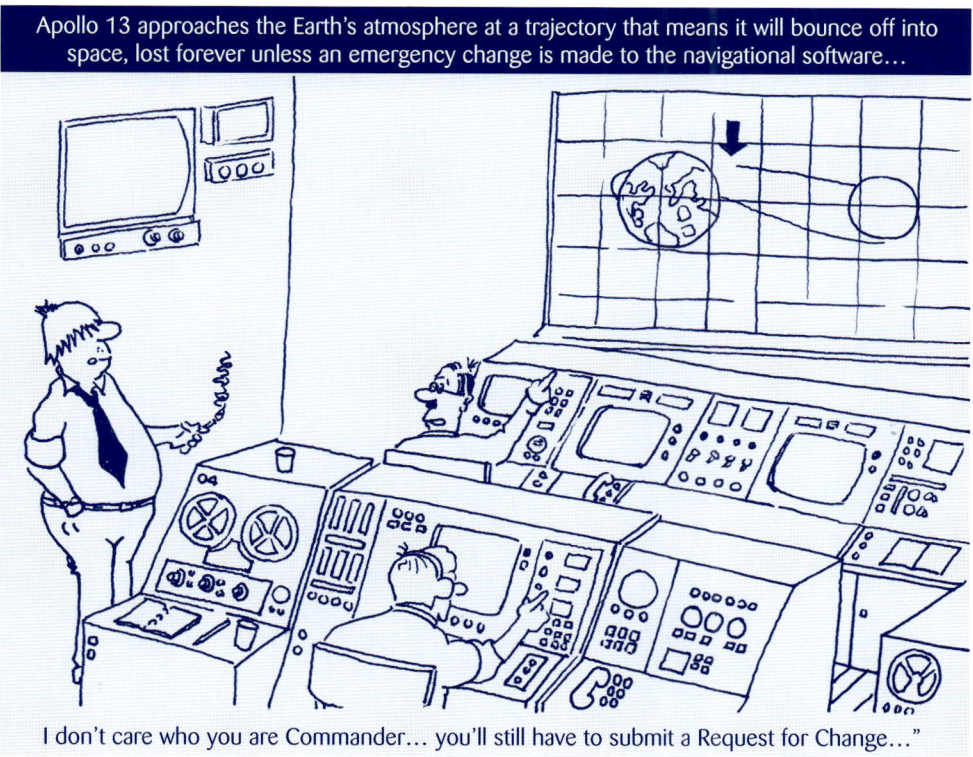

Apollo 13 approaches the Earth's atmosphere at a trajectory that means it will bounce off into space, lost forever unless an emergency change is made to the navigational software...

I don't care who you are Commander... you'll still have to submit a Request for Change..."

Or we implemented service level agreements; huge tomes of technology-focused statements and promises about bits & bytes, bandwidth, convoluted escalation mechanisms and availability formulas that could only be understood by quantum physicists. These were the good old days of the old economy. Sadly, these are no longer adequate in the new economy.

The new economy demands that we are more focussed on the 'tactical' processes. Business users start demanding things like service level agreements matched to business needs, using terminology and language that the business understands; guaranteeing availability of mission critical functionality, not of systems and platforms; faster more flexible change procedures; and flexible capacity management capable of absorbing the unpredictable demands of an unseen mass of internet users...

They start moaning about response times and performance and have finally cottoned on to the fact that 'a short wait will occur' was Bill Gates's idea of a joke.

We used to focus on tweaking systems to squeeze out some form of barely acceptable level of performance or install performance monitoring systems that captured and analysed anything that moved(consuming so much processing power and resources that user transactions didn't get a look in). These systems served simply to confirm what users could have told us for free. Performance sucks. In the new economy we are expected to build 'scalability' into systems, plan for capacity and match demands to expected internet usage and uptake.

The technical support chaps began to suspect that telling customers that systems would be restored within 30 minutes was not the good idea it seemed to be

What's so different about the Internet user?

This is an altogether strange new breed of creature that has evolved. It used to be that the only members of society that bought and used PCs were geeks or PC nerds . They would drool over the PC and delight in exploring it's inner software, or they would play games with the things. Now the majority of people with PCs are no longer interested in the PC itself or how it works. It is simply a way of getting onto the internet to surf for porn, jokes and free software.

More of them now are actually buying products (books and CDs) or using services (on-line banking, obtaining insurance policies or booking holidays). These cyber consumers want their transactions to be quick, easy and reliable. However, the technoids at the other end are all building web-sites that they think are state-of-the-art and aesthetically pleasing, using the latest multimedia technology to build all-singing and dancing front-ends which simply make things slower, are generally more confusing, and worse still, built on the back of legacy infrastructures held together by duck-tape and supported by the grunting, snorting, neanderthal technoid we have come to know and love.

Good sentence that one.

There is one significant difference between the traditional user of IT (the in-house victim that has nowhere else to go) and the cyber consumer. The cyber consumer, if pissed off, will simply not come back again.

Technoids have capital value

Experts predict the current shortage in IT skills will continue to grow at an ever more alarming rate as more and more businesses adopt IT to e-nable them. Experts predict new sourcing models as a solution. More technology expertise will be 'hired as needed'. In-house IT expertise will become more focused on managing IT supplier relationships. Business intelligence, service management and project management expertise will become more important for core, in-house staff.

At last! The business wallahs will realise they really do need us! In knowledge management terms this means that the value of the in-house IT staff as 'human capital' will grow and business continuity and growth will rely on the capabilities of those staff to adequately manage the portfolio of services and the partners in the delivery model. If we stay quiet we will be able to get away with even more.

Technoids as Knowledge workers

Technoids are evolving fairly rapidly up the evolutionary chain. In the pre-historic era when mainframes ruled the earth, technoids were known as tape monkeys. They lived in sealed-off environments and weren't let out of their cages.

In the desktop era they became known as the professional 'PC nerds'. They had to socialise with users. This meant that they had to learn to read and write and develop their first form of technobabble in an attempt to converse with users.

In the networked economy, IT is becoming all pervasive (judging by the most popular usage of the internet, we'd be inclined to say more 'perversive') . The increasing complexity and reach of IT has raised the technoid's status to that of IT specialist or cyber geek. They are expected to understand about society in general and how the great mass of unwashed humanity (that's you) are now their customers through the internet.

Business is expected to facilitate and speed up technoid evolution through continual investment in IT knowledge and by enabling them to capture and share experiences though Knowledge-based tools.

Suppliers

We saw that business managers are taking more interest in IT. Particularly IT failures (as these are more frequent than successes). Business managers want to know where the blame lies for hugely embarrassing, massively costly IT failures. The IT manager should take advantage of the business demands that we establish sourcing strategies to strategically select delivery chain partners.

What happened to tactics? No idea mate.

However, this usual failure to communicate will provide us with a good scapegoat. In our publication, 'Project management: what's all that about then?', we identified the need to have a handy scapegoat available when the sticky brown stuff hits the fan. Suppliers are an excellent scapegoat for IT and in fact we can point out that the business drove us into their waiting wallets!

In a recent Dutch IT study, it was revealed that IT managers were firing 3 out of 5 of their suppliers... (our publication was a popular seller in the Netherlands...maybe Dutch IT managers took our advice seriously).

Chapter five: Implementing ITIL (not)

IT organisations are being forced to improve the quality of their services, sadly. Now that the business has finally recognized that they need IT, failures and outages become visible and expose IT organisations to serious reflection and piss-taking within the business community, somebody has got to take the blame. We have read that the IT director seems to be a genetically perfect fit for the role. So how do we pass the buck? Blame the suppliers...

How not to implement ITIL

IT managers are being forced towards best practice approaches to help them improve service quality. ITIL is seen by many as the silver bullet to improve the quality of IT service delivery.

"I'd like to buy some ITIL"; "Install ITIL for me". People seem to think it is some kind of magic solution they can install in a day and then all will be well again.

We saw in chapter two (the IT growth/change model) that many IT organisations are still facing the shift from being an IT-focused product/service organisation (technoids that grunt and snort a lot) to becoming a more customer-focused organisation driven by SLA's (please note the mis-used apostrophe is back after a short holiday in The Netherland's. One or two smartarse's pointed out the mis-use of the apostrophe, failing to recognise that that this under-privileged little fella would be out of a job if not mis-used by IT illiterate's. Consequently he left in a fit of pique for a sojourn in The Netherland's where he could be employed in new ways such as s'Gravenhaag and van t'Veen without ridicule and letters to the editor).

Anyway.

The shift to mission critical use of IT demands that IT is even more business-focused:

• on the one hand, helping advise the business on the effective use of IT to support business goals (snigger)
• on the other, demonstrating that IT delivers business value.

Indeed the business is demanding that IT managers string whole sentences together. IT managers the world over are being confronted with strange words like 'startegy','stragety' or 'strategy' or whatever...). All part of aligning business and IT of course....

The ITIL bullet

So the silver bullet that is ITIL is often fired at us to get us all in line. This is a very dangerous time for the IT director. One thing people must realize is that when they make a decision to implement ITIL they are embarking on a program of organisational change. Implementing ITIL means reorganising the way in which the technoids work. It involves discipline and structure. This type of change by its very nature is prone to difficulties. People like us technoids generally don't like to change. We must show resistance and must rise up in opposition, placing the IT director between a rock (the business) and a hard place (us). Which is why the IT director needs to find a supplier to take the blame.

Terminology

Another reason the business likes ITIL is that it provides a common terminology. A terminology we can use in front of customers, terminology they can understand. Well, 'Sod off' is terminology that they understand too.

The general result is that the IT specialist blames the user for not being IT literate. Rightly or wrongly, this is an attitude that exists (rightly!!!!) and ITIL is seen as a step in the direction of communicating in terms the users understand.

.....service levels
.....business continuity
.....managing changes to the systems
.....maintaining workload throughput
.....guaranteeing availability
.....proactively work to prevent problems and speed up the time to deal with incidents and
     requests for service (yeah, right....)

How to let it all go belly up and still come out smelling of roses

We've noticed that very often the ITIL approach taken by an organisation falls into one of the following four categories - each one displaying visible (or should that be risible?) examples of IT staff making efforts to be professional, each one failing spectacularly to interpret what the business needs:

1. ITIL for the sake of ITIL. Everybody else is doing it, we should too. Then we can put a certificate on our wall saying we are ITIL certified. Having it is more important that what you do with it (tell that to the wife ....). So what if the quality of service hasn't improved? We've got ITIL now! We've got documented procedures and repeatable processes that explain how we manage to consistently deliver bad service. This is ITIL as a goal.

2. The second one is similar but has even more characteristics of fanaticism. ITIL is the holy grail. It's teachings are holy, they must be followed to the letter. That's what it says in the book, therefore that's the way it has to be done.

3. The third is the tool hunt, driven from the technology-based maturity level and approach to IT services. This is the attitude that a tool will solve all problems. Buy an expensive service management tool and install ITIL on it and everything will improve.

4. The fourth way is really an amalgamation of the others. Produce masses of reports based upon what it says in the ITIL books. Or base reports on examples taken from other ITIL implementations to save time. Reports so detailed, so thick, so meaningless it costs a fortune to produce them. Everybody is too embarrassed to ask the question, 'Yes but what do the bloody things tell me?'.

ITIL as the goal

What seems to be positive is that we have a goal. ITIL is the goal, everybody goes on ITIL training. People are indoctrinated into ITIL ways and terminology. ITIL process flows and procedures are made and proudly shown. Process owners are established (ownership being the characteristic of dumping it somewhere lower in the organisation). There is a distinct lack of real ownership, sponsorship or commitment from above. There is a distinct lack of any form of goal alignment with strategic goals of the IT organisation because of the lack of sponsorship or top level ownership.

Furthermore, people responsible, be it operational managers or process owners, or people er, somewhere else, don't know what the goals of the process are. Generally a bloody good thing too for us; we need more people obsessed with ITIL as a goal in itself so that the activities taking place bear little resemblance to enabling the goal or demonstrating the result. When the buck needs passing, we can blame the business for not having clearly defined goals.

We pinned down one IT director who described his goal. One of the main business issues was that changes never got carried out on time. It appeared that identifying this problem *unequivocally* was one of the goals the IT director set when deciding to implement ITIL Change Management. No effort was expended on impact assessment of changes or change scheduling, or indeed on the evaluation of a change (to identify the bottlenecks or improve planning changes). The reports confirmed that, indeed, changes were not meeting planning requirements and were never on time....

You'd have to have a heart of stone not to piss yourself laughing.

ITIL to the letter

ITIL to the letter is very similar. This is where people carry ITIL books around in their pockets and smugly quote huge tracts whenever confronted by any doubts or questions about its relevance to the organisation. This in part leads to the often-used rejoinder that ITIL was written when Dinosaurs ruled the Earth. (Dinosaurs being mainframes. A metaphor. Hilarious, eh?)

This type of organisation wants to IMPLEMENT ITIL. These people make fundamentalists look reasonable. Fanatics run away when they have to converse with these followers of the ITIL.

'That's what it says in the book'. How often have you heard that?

The subtext here is 'It's more than my job's worth (not to follow procedures)'.

This type of approach demands procedures. Thousands of them. Procedures are described in handbooks and all too often the authors see them as great literary productions. The authors believe that great literary works are thick, and therefore handbooks and procedures should also be thick.

And so should the audience. That's us, that is.

The good thing about this approach is that whenever the business starts requesting changes or trying to raise incidents, we ensure they have to read and follow detailed procedures and complete forms in triplicate before we even consider doing anything for them. When this all goes wrong we can blame ITIL for being out-dated and too inflexible.

I followed the **ITIL** procedures and according to me you are now a satisfied customer!...

A fool with a tool...

'A fool with a tool is still a fool' declare business managers smugly, when they hear we IT professionals are installing a new systems and service management tool to help us to effectively and efficiently (see earlier) support their IT services. What they forget is that some fool in the business signed off on the budget to allow us to buy it in the first place, so who's the fool now dip-stick? Er, sorry about that, of course we mean that we are very grateful for the signature.

The fact that some sort of tool is necessary to manage today's complex ICT infrastructures is now generally taken as a no-brainer. As is the fact that those signatories to our business cases believe anything we tell them as long as we mention efficiency and effectiveness.

We suggest also that you formulate a vision statement for IT based on *'Your mission Jim, should you accept it, is to boldy go and seek out IT components in the dark recesses of the user community, to discover them and bring them under Starfleet (corporate IT) control.'* Of course you don't publish quite like that. You publish *'Our mission is to increase efficiency and effectiveness'.*

As an IT professional, your job is not necessarily to obtain a tool that is fit for purpose. Your job is to create a Command and Control centre (sexy military phrase and very macho) or a Mission Control Bridge (very futuristic and science fiction, high-techy image). These are basically large areas filled with bleeping, blipping, flashing lights and consoles with multi coloured display screens that you can proudly show off to visitors.

As ever where men are involved, it is a sign of virility to have the biggest Distributed Infrastructure Control & Knowledge centre (DICK).

And as IT professional head of the centre who understands the whole technical shooting match, you can proudly live up to the title already informally used to refer to you in the business community............DICKhead.

You must of course request more staff to fill the banks of consoles, claim more ICT budget and expand your IT empire, then train them up to say *'Aye, aye Cap'n. Warp factor 5 it is'*, man it with strange beings who speak in a dialect that nobody can understand (technobabble), preferably allied to weird behavioural traits of the type Spock made famous (particularly that much prized user unfriendly behaviour) so that your DICK can be pretty much like most IT support centres throughout the world.

When the tool approach goes wrong we can of course blame the tool suppliers for selling us something we didn't need or for not aligning it to our process needs.

Reports should reflect ongoing goals and priority service improvement issues. Finding content in the reports that actually underpin the required goals of the implementation of ITIL is often difficult. If you do find it, make sure the process of finding somebody charged with the responsibility of actually doing something with the reports leads the buggers round in circles.

If you have more than the requisite number of brain cells needed to work in IT, you will remember the growth/change model for IT organisations (the shift from technology-based products and services to a more customer-focused approach). An often forgotten issue in ITIL implementations is the customer. Improvement goals are very often set from the perspective of, and in consultation with, the IT organisation.

And we need to keep it that way.

The Fourth way

Sounds like a new age religion. The Fourth way! Or maybe another means of carrying out the death penalty in Aghanistan after stoning, beheading, and boring with marathon readings of *'What women can't do here, so there'*. Anyway it's a combination of the other three so we can just leave it there.

One way of ensuring your ITIL improvement program fails is to create a project to carry it through. Inevitably there will be a battle between the 'line' organisation and the 'project' organisation as to who has access to which poor unfortunate technoid. They'll never be able to agree or give an inch. The result will be that nothing will get done.

Symeonides began to worry that being the best resource in the office would not always work to his advantage

Prompted by more of those management and business consultants (the very ones that sold the promised riches that business process re-engineering would bring), business managers are now starting to ask questions about the IT value chain (see earlier wise words).

Is IT a ball and chain around our necks? Is IT holding us back from the promised land? Is there really an IT value chain waiting to be realised?

The IT value chain?

Yes. So what? Back to the value chain, it being:

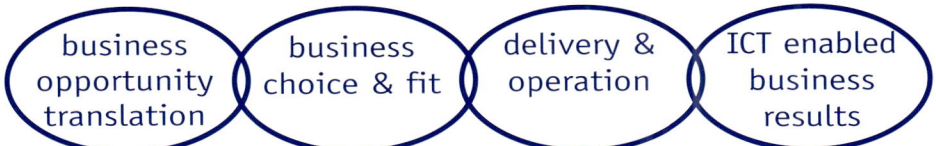

business opportunity translation · business choice & fit · delivery & operation · ICT enabled business results

Business now expects IT to demonstrate the value chain. The piles of meaningless reports we generally fob off on them are no longer adequate. They want a scorecard containing a set of key steering indicators. IT managers must get themselves ready to blind them with science and here is an approach that works.

Launch a program called MIUAYG

Management **I**nformation **U**nderpinning **A**greed **Y**early **G**oals (what it really means is **M**ake **I**t **U**p **A**s **Y**ou **G**o) a programme designed to produce IT steering information.

Central to the MIUAYG is a graph that shows the 'BS' index. As far as the business is concerned we tell them this is a 'Business Service' index. A set of indicators based upon a complex algorithm (too complex to explain to them), agreed with business unit managers. Preferably one or two of the business unit managers who cower in your presence and would do anything to please you just so long as you let them keep their PCs, or won't split on for downloading porn). The BS indicator shows the aggregated index of IT added value performance. It is made up of:

- total cost reduction index
- business revenue guess-timate which indicates IT % contribution to revenue generation weighted against business process performance, product sales and business-to-customer-functional interaction
- cycle time for business functional IT realisation
- satisfaction indicator weighted against business quality criteria.

It's just a way of showing a line on a graph that rises or falls as we see fit, but it makes it look as though we've really thought about it and aligned it to business thingies. And it sounds fantastic.

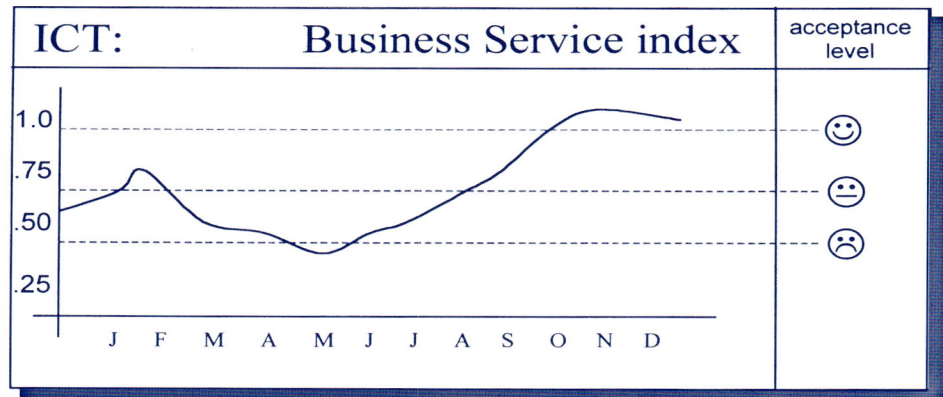

The Balanced scorecard

This is another popular performance measurement framework that causes business managers to wet themselves with glee (even though they don't understand anything other than the 'Financial' element). Here is a balanced scorecard we set up as a joke that a business manager thought was real. He declared that if the IT organisation could meet the targets it would be a major leap forward-presumably from living in caves and clubbing animals and PCs to death.

Financial
%   IT budget spent on things other than beer & pizzas

%   Value of ITC organisation in relation to a set of Pokemon cards

Customer
%   decrease in amount of users physically or verbally abused by the help desk

%   increase in users actually ABLE to login in the morning

Internal
%   ITC personnel that can formulate sentences and that can speak without grunting

%   changes the user community were aware of BEFORE the systems crashed AGAIN as a result of an unplanned change

Innovation
%   of ICT systems not glued, nailed, tied with string or stuck together by duck tape or chewing gum

Both of these frameworks look good but are in fact totally useless. And that leads us to the next chapter. What is the most useful thing that we in IT can design and implement and that we need to disable into utter uselessness asap? It's...

With the right attitude (a bad one), the right tools (the wrong ones that is), the right people (technoids, sub-humans, sociopaths or serial killers) and an intrinsic contempt for customers, you too can have an IT helpdesk. Or Service Desk, to quote the new ITIL (name changed to pretend it is a new concept of course).

In the past we contented ourselves with defining worst practice around telephone answering, but some fools ignored our advice to restrict the bastards to using the phone and allowed customers to become familiar with technology such that they now can use e-mail. And that means we need to review our earlier good advice (the justly infamous 'NOT the ITIL' publication) and explain to you how to be as unhelpful as possible using any communication channel.

We really must say it's not easy being advisors in the face of such foolishness, but if we don't do it, where will things end? Customers will be demanding not just action, but results and we will not be able to get away with the action being to throw something in the bin and the result being that nothing happens.

Old advice about chucking away anything that customers were stupid enough to write down and send does still apply, but some smart arses have been defining standards for document record management (easy to knacker) and electronic records management. Tricky, that one.

…but that's because customers are too ignorant to understand the longer dynamics… I think we need to find the sort of customer that appreciates our vision!…

Customer satisfaction

Worst practice

As always, it is best to take advice from those who know. We have commissioned new (hah!) advice from our teams of Help desk and Service desk consultants and come up with fresh (hah!) advice from around the globe and from many different organisations those wanting to sell something. Our first piece comes from an organisation that came in for a bit of bad press (particularly from a well-known superpower). They also came in for a bit of a slapping as they say down in cockney circles. Let's just call them the T******. Being on the receiving end of such bad press, they decided to create a Help desk (they are of course rather set in their ways and do not feel comfortable with the modernity of 'Service desk'.

■ After receiving ITIL-aid (a new concept for those who cannot afford ITIL consultants), their advisors er, advised that because of their, er, unusual attitude to the female sex (even by the standards set by the average IT wallah), separate Help desks to take calls from men and women might be appropriate.

The severity levels and FAQs/Action lists are included here for you to copy as you wish. Or not.

All calls must be assigned a severity level as described below.

Severity 1 = Will result in eternal damnation

Severity 2 = Will result in civil war

Severity 3 = Would prevent the propagation of the holy race

Severity 4 = Would be quite embarrassing for the men in the family

Severity 5 = Doesn't matter a damn actually but why let the bitches have any pleasure

Record details of the call type on the bits of paper hanging on the side of your camel. Example calls are described below.

Call type	Action
How can I get a career	Xfer call directly to husband or father or brother
How can I get a bacon sandwich	Xfer call directly to husband or father or brother
How can I get a pair of jeans	Xfer call directly to amputation/flagellation section
How can I get a leg wax	Xfer call directly to husband or father or brother
How can I get an orgasm	Xfer call directly to amputation and arrange for immediate removal of her tongue filthy bitch
How can I get a plane ticket out of here	Xfer call directly to amputation/flagellation section
How can I get educated	Xfer call directly to husband or father or brother
How can I get a vibrator	Xfer call directly to husband or father or brother
How can I get a bank account	Xfer call directly to amputation/flagellation section
How can I get contraception	See orgasm
How can I get a chance to fight the capitalist pigs in the west	Xfer call directly T****** Help Desk - Male Section (but tell husband or father at same time)
Wrong number from male caller	Remind him of the terrors of eternal damnation and xfer to correct help desk.

All calls must be assigned a severity level as described below.

Severity 1 = Will result in killing Western pigs

Severity 2 = Will result in hurting Western pigs

Severity 3 = Might embarrass Western pigs

Severity 4 = Would be quite embarrassing for the donkeys owned by Western pigs

Severity 5 = Doesn't matter a damn; we are men

Record details of the call type on the bits of paper hanging on the side of your camel. Example calls are described below.

Call type	Action
How can I get a career	Join the Jihad
How can I get a bacon sandwich	Kill the Western pigs
How can I get a pair of jeans	Kill the Western pigs
How can I kill a Western pig	Er, that was join the Jihad...
How can I join a Jihad	Get a false beard on this man at once
How can I get to spiritual enlightenment	Learn to fly
How can I get to heaven	Ah, that's join the Jihad again
How can I get a wife	Xfer call directly to husband or father or brother of women on our books
How can I get stoned	Any more questions like this and you'll find out mate
How can I get contraception	Stone the infidel
Bush on the line for Mullah Omar	Explain that God is just about fed up with him and any time now, probably in the next few seconds (or maybe later) He is going to smite him pretty hard. Or not. As God wills. But probably.
Wrong number from a female	Cut off the ears and tear out the tongue of the bitch for talking to a man who is not her husband, father or brother.

We'd like to think that we can all learn a lot from that lot.

Nuclear Energy Service desk

One of the finest Service desks in Australia, the Nuclear Energy desk, boasted up-to-the-minute software, highly trained, ITIL qualified operators, state-of-the-art furnishings and, as it was in Australia, fridges packed with Fosters and XXXX.

Their finest moment arrived when the whole shooting match went into meltdown. Even under the duress of knowing that most of the desert in which the plant sat would soon be ....desert, but ....more so, the brave operator followed procedure to the letter. We quote from monitored phone logs.

Operative *'G'day, Nuclear Energy Service desk, Kylie speaking, how can I help you?'*

Caller *'It's..'*

Actually that *was* it but the polite greeting and total failure to actually do anything is an example to us all. OK, we admit that there wasn't a great lot young Kylie could have done, but that does not mean we should assume she would have done anything anyway.

Of other interest is that the Business Continuity Plan (and the Contingency plans and Risk logs) were all kept with the porn in the cupboard under the reactor. Mind you as they had been copied from the backs of various old ITIL books, updated when someone invented a 'new' way of doing things and then submitted to the sub-group for rural research for benchmarking crappy plans, we doubt that they were missed. Unlike Kylie.

Service desk greetings

Say what you will about the Police (and we do), the best new advice on service desk greetings comes from the Old Bill.

Operative *'Hello, hello, hello'.*

Sure beats the Bomb squad automated response system

Press 1 if you have cut the green wire
Press 2 if you have cut the red wire
Press 3, oh you cut the black one, well in that case kiss your arse goodbye.

A recent article in New Scientist suggests that in Germany they intend to transplant the brain stem cells of pigs into humans. We wondered where they will find the coppers to volunteer.

Chapter eight: Knackering change

Having recognised that 'Implementing ITIL' is, to a large extent, an issue of managing organisational change, we in IT need a worst practice approach to making change happen badly. So we need to know where these bloody change theorists are coming from.

Transformation theorists have done a great deal of the ground work for us and told us exactly where we will probably fail, so that when we do actually succumb to their predictions and warnings, they can say 'we told you so', 'we told you that you *needed* us'. Back in the mists of time (54 BC), the prophet Elijah Kotter defined eight steps for transforming the organisation.

Step	Tips for success
Create a sense of urgency	Tell people 'This change is very important. Let me put it another way; if it doesn't work you're all fired!'
Form a guiding coalition; a group with enough power to lead the change effort	Find yourself a group of scapegoats and 'yesmen' to goad into doing what you want.
Creating a vision, to help direct the change effort	Create yourself a vision of change such that nobody really knows what it means in terms of real change, particularly change as in jobs will go. E.g. 'there will be new challenging opportunities for all employees' (being able to sign on is a challenging opportunity).
Communicate the vision	Communicate in terms open to any manner of interpretations, such that you can't be pinned down to any specific, concrete meaning.
Empowering others to act on the vision	Find yourself a group of scapegoats who you can blame if things go wrong, arm them with enough authority to kick the organisation around, but not enough authority to be able to turn on you.
Planning for and creating short term wins	If jobs are to go, capitalise on the opportunity for sacking awkward, objectional managers to show that even the management team must make sacrifices.
Consolidating improvements and producing still more change	Kick them when they're down.
Institutionalise new approaches	Ensure that feedback is given on people failing to follow procedures, make examples of them and sack them.

COMPANY RULES
1. The Company Director is ALWAYS right
2. IF the Company Director is wrong, see rule 1

Company rules

selection

I see you've changed the selection criteria for new middle managers...

'must be yes men...'
'must be willing to accept blame on behalf of the boss...'
'...the ability to unashamedly grovel to the boss...'

Elijah chipped out the words describing the eight steps onto some paving stones and tried selling them to the people of the Netherlands as the *eight paving stones covered with wise words that you should use to transform business*. However, business in the Netherlands was restricted in those days to the odd plague cure, cheese making and, of course, pornography.

And the eight steps were thought to be a little radical for the fledgling porn industry, particularly as they did not solve the problem of the artists used to depict the live sex shows being unable to complete a canvas before the models died of exhaustion.

Elijah smashed up the paving stones in frustration and his dad used the pieces to make up a lovely crazy-paved pathway in front of their brothel in Amsterdam.

Fortunately for the world, a descendant of Elijah, John Kotter, found the stones when he was digging a leek trench in the garden and put the pieces back together. The world at last would know the Kotter vision!

Face to two-faced communication can be very trying for the IT manager. More often than not you are faced by some imbecile whom you suspect can barely master his or her natural language and considers it a personal achievement to make whole sentences. Nevertheless 'interpersonal communication' must be attempted.

Culture

Culture is a very tricky, soft, gooey issue that many people think is best avoided. You can't change a culture overnight. Or, if you are Australian, in 250 years. So ignore it.

The emotions of change

Transformation theorists have taken a long hard look at both the history of change and the development of resistance to change and started identifying some trends relating to the way that people react and the way that they behave. This naturally led to the creation of some buzzwords, the odd model or two and the construction of some (ir)rational theory to explain it all. Basically, what they are trying to con us all into believing is that people are not just simply being bloody awkward. They're being bloody awkward within the boundaries of some 'model'.

The penalty for resisting change seemed unduly severe to Wheeldon

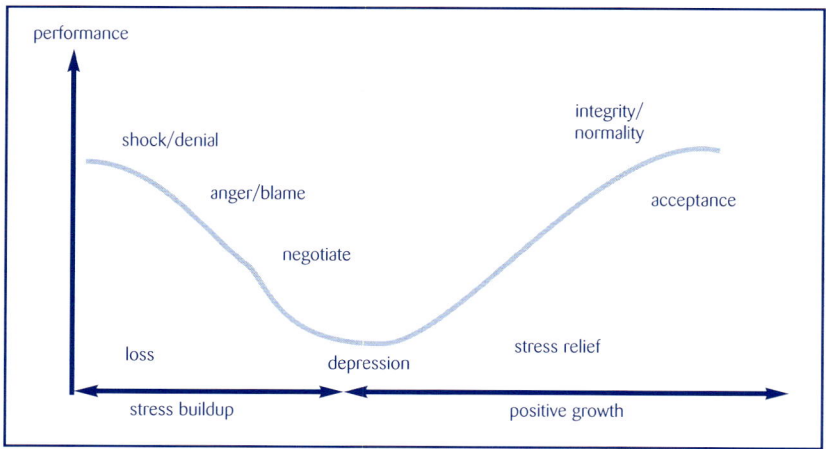

What they are saying is that when you, in your infinite wisdom, armed with superior intellect and self righteousness, proudly launch your logically supported initiative of change, the very people who you are trying to change will first go through the following phases:

Phase	Characteristics
Shock and denial	• it can't be! • they can't do that! • I don't believe they'll do it • It's a mistake, they'll soon realise… • not with Camilla, surely!
Anger and blame	• they can't be allowed to get away with this • it's her fault… • we're not putting up with this… • we'll show them… • we'll get our own back • I did not have sex with that woman!!!!!
Negotiation	• pretending it's not going to happen • clinging on to old ways • searching for compromises • how much to keep it out of the papers?
Depression	• lack of motivation • lack of energy • grudging acceptance and realisation • suicide
Acceptance of the new order	• looking forward instead of desperately clinging on to the old • searching for new values • new enthusiasm • yes dear, I will do the washing and the ironing and the cleaning
Integration and normality	• the new becomes the normal way of doing things • so it's settled, we can now occupy Poland

Ratcliffe illustrated the likely reception awaiting those wishing to implement ideas picked up from *it*SMF conferences.

Business Strategy

Which of these statements most applies to your IT organsation's view of the Business strategy and how it includes IT

- What Business are we in? ❑

- What's a Business? ❑

- You mean we've got a Business strategy? ❑

- The Business strategy is to make life as difficult as possible for the IT organisation by not making any decisions, changing their minds every 10 minutes and refusing to accept advice. ❑

- The Business strategy statement declares IT is a mission critical Business enabler. IT has the full commitment from the business (providing they don't ask for any money, resources, time, attention and input from the business). ❑

Steering IT

How competent is the Business in steering IT?

- If they knew what IT stood for it would be a start ❑

- Some of our managers know somebody who once saw a PC, which now makes them experts in making IT decisions ❑

- If they could remember their passwords it would be an improvement. ❑

- They think that the Internet is still just hype ❑

- Some of them actually know how to get past the screen saver ❑

Business added value of IT

How does the IT organisation add value?

- The IT organisation is a black hole of investment, where nothing of value ever comes out. ❑

- Our IT organisation adds value to society. (We employ the dregs of society that nobody else in their right mind would employ!). ❏

- We'd get more value out of our IT employees by swapping them for a set of Pokemon cards. ❏

- Our IT demonstrably improves the effectiveness and efficiency of business operations....then I woke up and realised it was a dream. ❏

IT Strategic direction

Which of these statements most applies to your Business view of the 'IT strategy'?

- What another strategy? Again? I'm sure I've heard of that word somewhere? ❏

- If they could spell strategy I'd be impressed ❏

- They say they have a strategy but it's far too complicated to explain to us... we should just let them get on with it ❏

- Their strategy is to seek out and implement technology solutions that are no use to man nor beast in this organisation ❏

- Their strategy is to boldly go where no IT organisation has gone before... and to cock it up BIG time ❏

Business IT needs

Which of the following statements best identifies the Business IT needs (according to the Business)?

- Customer Relationship management supporting technology & systems ❏

- Knowledge management infrastructure ❏

- improved corporate & global communications via Internet & Intranet technology ❏

- E-Business enablement ❏

- Any of the above, providing it doesn't cost us anything ❏

*Which of the following statements best identifies the Business IT needs
(according to the IT Organisation)?*

- One or more of the above (as if), so long as it doesn't cost anything and they
  can have it tomorrow ❏

- Internet access so that they can download all those 'naughty' pictures
  (you won't find anyone in IT doing that sort of thing) ❏

- The ability to chat to total strangers on the other side of the planet about
  weird, obscure hobbies that normal people aren't interested in ❏

- The ability to download flashy screen savers to impress their friends....
  (or rather people they know, friends is going a bit far) and to download
  as much 'free software' as possible, despite the fact that they haven't
  got a clue as to how it works ❏

- To hunt out & download the latest, most destructive virus on the internet and
  then to mail it to everybody ❏

- The ability to send 'free' electronic greetings cards so that they don't
  have to pay any money...tight fisted gits...they won't invest a cent in new IT ❏

Systems

*Which of these statements best describes your organisation's approach to managing information with
systems?*

- We use bits of paper with joined up forms of writing ❏

- We have standard forms for recording ignorance and make basic use of PCs
  for things other than playing games and installing trendy screen savers ❏

- We have corporate information systems with complex security codes that
  exclude everybody ❏

- Anything that moves is turned into an information system that is openly
  and widely available to all those that don't need it ❏

- We have a corporate database with meaningless search algorithms and search
  keys to ensure that nobody can find the knowledge they need ❏

- We have intranets, extranets, internets and any other kind of net we can use for
  plugging our PCs into for flooding the rest of the world with ignorance ❏

Innovation

Which of the following statements best reflects your organisation's approach to dealing with innovation?

- A new idea from IT? Chance would be a fine thing ❏

- I once had a new idea but it gave me a headache so I had to lie down and have a rest. Fortunately when I woke up again it had gone and so had my headache ❏

- New IT ideas are dangerous. They are very likely to rock the boat, cause us work... and cost money ❏

- New IT ideas are ignored until they go away by themselves ❏

- New ideas are enthusiastically received and are then just as enthusiastically ignored ❏

- New ideas are carefully analysed, matched to our strategic intentions, feasibility studied, piloted and then discarded because they are out of date ❏

IT competence

How does the IT organisation manage its competencies?

- They send technoids on obscure courses that are of little value, where they can get together to grunt at each other ❏

- Recruitment & selection procedures ensure that the right type of person is captured...before the police can get them ❏

- It's strictly on the job learning...play with it, cock it up and then hand it over to the business ❏

- They go on management training where they learn how to produce reports in gobbledygook ❏

Business value creation

How does the Business create value from IT?

- We should consider outsourcing the business to another IT services organisation ❏

- Value??? All they ever do is whinge and moan, change their minds, ask for systems faster than a speeding bullet... ❏

You may have noticed that we have not followed the new ITIL approach to updating better (or in our case, worst) practice. Indeed not. We have in fact come up with some new ideas and words. Yes, we have used words we used before, such as 'the' 'and' and 'bugger' to name but three. However—-and this is the hairdressing bit science fans—-we have not simply rearranged the order of the words, but we have written some things you haven't read before!

Not only that, but we have succeeded in improving our worst practice! And we aren't offensive to women any more (well, ok we are personally, but we now realise that women deserve a place in IT and we are happy to admit we were wrong and take them back as our secretaries).

The new ITIL can be used to knacker change effectively by telling the business that you need a pile of dosh to do it all again slightly differently starting from scratch because ITIL was not quite right between, ooohh about 1996 and 2000 or so, because no one took any notice of business drivers since they were too busy pushing leading edge issues such as....... Well, there was a book on ITIL in small organisations, but that sort of edited old stuff and said it was 'a good idea' for small organisations, so that was something, and there was a book about, well, er, interviewing, and, er, recognising that problems existed (that's a good bit, honest), and erm, oh yes, a really good bit where it points out that all staff should be aware of the core business activities and aims of the organisation they are a part of. Ideally, that was (past tense, old book, 1997). The book was not suggesting that this was compulsory or anything like that.

Laugh? We thought we'd never start.

It was also marvellous about stuff like how to use a whiteboard and that handouts were really quite a good idea. Oh yes, it did suggest that if you wrote stuff down, you could prioritise tasks by writing 1,2,3, etc (the etc was very important in case you forgot there were more than three numbers in the, erm, alphabet we suppose). It also pointed out in detail (more really good cutting edge stuff) that this work was best done at the end of one day and suggested you use the title, 'Jobs to do tomorrow'. What's really brilliant is that if you failed to follow this sage advice and made your list at the start of the next day, to save confusion it suggested you could use the title, 'Jobs to do today'!

In case you think we are making this up, we would like to quote (verbatim) a particularly plangent paragraph from this work:

There are very few situations where a snap decision is required, except where there is immediate danger to yourself or others, and in such cases it is often better to trust and act according to your basic instincts and experience than to deliberate too long and perish doing so.'

Now, who says that IT people don't have insight?

It is tempting to provide you with the ISBN number for this work of genius, but you would probably try to buy it instead of this book because it is funnier.

Suffice to say it was edited in the wilderness years but CCTA should still take a lot of the blame. An apology would have been nice.

Actually, we can't leave that book without stealing another nugget; apparently, best practice used to be that if there was not a clock in the room, you had to look at your watch. Some things just cannot be improved on can they?

I think, therefore I am an ITIL guru

We would like to think that the last few hundred words illustrate that you can put old medicine in new bottles and make it worthwhile. And pretty much all ITIL experts do exactly that (but with a surprising absence of humour, invention or anything approaching innovation). So really, it's up to you to work out how to knacker change more effectively (and efficiently).

All we can do is try to put you on the wrong road and trust it doesn't work out.

If in doubt, consult any of the tomes from the wilderness years. You will need little else to ensure that nothing you do will be taken seriously ever again and no other help to perpetuate eternal chaos in any change programme you wish to scupper.

However, if you want the good stuff ....

Service Support	ISBN 0 113 300 158
Service Delivery	ISBN 0 113 300 174
Planning to Implement Service Management	ISBN 0 113 308 779
Applications Management	ISBN 0 113 308 663
ICT Infrastructure Management	ISBN 0 113 308 655
The Business Perspective	ISBN 0 113 308 949
Security Management	ISBN 0 113 300 14X

BS15000:2002

PD0005. A Code of Practice for IT Service Management	ISBN 0 580 295 826

Pocket Guide to IT Service Management   ISBN 0 952 470 616
(also in German (0 952 470 624, US English (0 952 470 632) & French (0 952 470 640))

Dictionary of Terms, Acronyms & Abbreviations   ISBN 0 952 470 659
(also in US English (0 952 470 667))

Not the IT Infrastructure Library	ISBN 0 953 346 900
Project management :what's all that about then?	ISBN 0 953 346 919
Ignorance management	ISBN 0 953 346 927

*it*SMF Ltd.

Webbs Court
8 Holmes Road
Earley
Reading RG6 7BH
United Kingdom
Tel: +44(0)118 926 0888
Fax: +44(0)118 926 3073
e-mail: service@itsmf.com
www.itsmf.com

OGC

Rosebery Court
St Andrews Business Park
Norwich NR7 0HS
United Kingdom
Tel: +44(0)1603 704567
Fax: +44(0)1603 704817
e-mail: info@ogc.gov.uk
www.ccta.gov.uk
www.itil.co.uk

British Standards Institution

389 Chiswick High Road
London W4 4AL
United Kingdom
Tel: +44(0)208 996 9001
Fax: +44(0)208 996 7001
e-mail: info@bsi-global.com
www.bsi-global.com

Giggle

Tel: +44 (0)1603 704315 (Brian)
Tel: +31 (0)79 3207779 (Paul)
http://web.inter.nl.net/users/pwilkins/

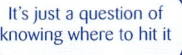